Secret dishes from around the world

£25.00

First published in 2019 by Bounceback Books
2 Federation Street
Manchester
M4 4BF
info@bouncebackfood.co.uk
www.bouncebackfood.co.uk

ISBN: 978-1-9162650-0-4

Text: Copyright © Duncan Swainsbury
Illustrations: © Libby Element
Graphic design by Peter Lang
Printed and bound by Ingram Spark, England

All proceeds from the sale of this book will help fund future Bounceback
Food CIC projects.

A CIP catalogue record of this book is available from the British Library.

SECRET

DISHES FROM AROUND THE WORLD

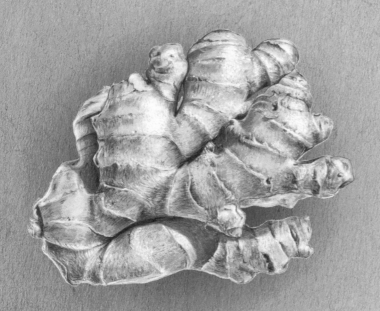

ACKNOWLEDGEMENTS

This recipe book is dedicated to Walter, the oldest member of our cookery school. His passion for cooking and his community spirit are a constant source of motivation.

We are also indebted to Libby Element, the Manchester-based artist who brought this book to life with her exceptional paintings.

Thank you to everyone who pledged their support as part of our 'Back the Book' crowdfunding campaign – we hope the book is worth the wait! Special mention must also go to:

Sarah Faulkner

Sarah held several bake sales in her office to fundraise for the book and has provided us with superb mentoring and support for the duration of the project.

Erin Elliot and David Morris

Erin and David are both honorary members of our cookery school and have been to several of our **buy one, give one** community cookery courses in Sandbach. They also helped out with recipe development and testing!

Newcastle University's Rise Up team, the School for Social Entrepreneurs and Unltd

Thank you for helping to guide the development of our organisation.

Our partner cookery workshop venues, foodbank collection points and distribution centres

Thank you for your support in our fight against food poverty, every step of the way.

DESIGN CREDITS

We'd also like to thank:

Michael Ainsworth

North or Nowt are a Leeds-based screen print and design studio, specialising in gig-poster printing for musical acts around the UK. They work with a variety of creatives to deliver fine art print projects.

North or Nowt have also worked with Bounceback by printing and supplying our t-shirts and aprons.

 www.northornowt.com

 north_or_nowt

Etsy etsy.com/uk/shop/NorthorNowt

Peter Lang

Peter is an experienced freelance graphic designer with over 10 years experience working in and around Greater Manchester.

He has helped to bring together the illustrations and exciting recipes that you will find in Bounceback's first recipe book.

 www.peterdoesdesign.co.uk

 peter@peterdoesdesign.co.uk

Welcome to our community cookery school

Thank you for purchasing a copy of our recipe book!

Not only have you got your hands on a selection of our favourite *Secret dishes from around the world,* you've also joined a growing number of people actively deciding to 'Buy social for a better world' – the theme of Social Enterprise UK's 2019 national campaign.

Social enterprises represent a different way of doing business. They are set up to address some of the most difficult challenges that face our society and give something back to their community.

Since starting out in 2014, Bounceback Food CIC has donated 9,000+ items of food and hygiene products to foodbanks and taught 1,000+ people how to cook healthy meals from around the world using the **buy one**, **give one** model.

Within our community cookery school, this means that every person who pays to join a course also funds a free place for somebody referred to us from a local foodbank or partner third sector organisation. We apply the same principle at market events, where we stock a range of pasta, rice, soup and tinned food: the same item bought by a member of the public is also donated to the nearest foodbank. This proactive approach to fighting food poverty has helped our non-profit social enterprise to build a core team of staff, volunteers and supporters based in Manchester – the home of doing things differently!

So thank you for remembering the power of your purchases and buying this recipe book. In doing so, you're helping us to scale up our social impact as we expand our outreach work into all 10 boroughs of Greater Manchester, Cheshire and North Wales.

We hope you enjoy making our favourite *Secret dishes from around the world!*

Happy cooking,
The Bounceback Team

CONTENTS

Vegetarian

Vegan

OUR STORY SO FAR...

June 2015

After trading regularly at
Altrincham Market, we reached
our first social impact target –
1,000 foodbank donations!

2014

November 2014

Bounceback Food CIC began life as
a Christmas market stall in Salford
where we first tested the **buy one,
give one** concept with a basic range
of pasta, rice and tinned food.

2015

December 2015

Shortly after our 1st birthday
we were asked to share
our story at TEDx Sheffield.

July 2016

By the summer of 2016, the donated food from our market events had contributed to over 10,000 meals in the North West!

September 2017

This was when we piloted our first **buy one**, **give one** cookery course in Altrincham. We've since expanded the concept to Knutsford, Sandbach, Wilmslow, Manchester and Salford!

2016   2017   2018

April 2017

As well as donating food to foodbanks, we started to teach people how to cook healthy nutritious meals, improve their budgeting skills and provide support with nutrition. By Easter 2017, we had taught our first 50 participants!

January 2018

A team of interns from Manchester Metropolitan University joined the Bounceback Food team for 2 months in our co-working office in Manchester. They were superb! We now run an annual social enterprise internship programme every summer.

2018

2019

June 2018

Using specially adapted kitchen equipment, we delivered our first cookery courses specifically designed for stroke survivors.

August 2018

Our 'Back the Book' crowdfunder launched! During the 2-week campaign, we successfully raised the £2,500 required to complete this book. Our selection of rewards included supper clubs, honorary memberships and our recently launched corporate Cook Off challenge.

March 2019

With our community cookery school in full swing, we reached another social impact milestone – over 1,000 people have now learnt to cook with us!

The Future

May 2019

We recently launched our Cooking and Nutrition Portal, which is giving individuals and organisations access to our range of healthy recipes, meal planning support, budgeting advice and nutritional guidance.

Future

Head to page 82 to see what we've got planned!

Duncan Swainsbury
FOUNDER

After spending time volunteering in a foodbank, I noticed that lorry loads of 'waste' food would arrive from supermarkets that couldn't necessarily be given to people in need. I also felt that the way that foodbank donation points in supermarkets were located and presented meant that they came across as an afterthought.

I wanted to set up an organisation that gave people the opportunity to make a conscious decision to support someone living in food poverty. Applying the **buy one, give one** model to the way in which people buy staple food and learn how to cook, has brought people together in their communities who may not have previously interacted. My goal is now to apply the concept across different sectors to fight poverty and inequality on multiple fronts.

FAVOURITE DISH

Red Lentil & Spinach Masala
(page 34)

Josh Rea
HEAD CHEF

I joined Bounceback Food CIC via their internship programme shortly after completing my degree in 2018. My main focus has been developing recipes and delivering cookery courses to a wide range of people in communities across Greater Manchester.

For me, meeting people from all walks of life and getting their perspective about food is something that makes working at Bounceback really great. No two cookery workshops are the same and it's inspiring to see people's confidence and relationship with food develop over time. I think people benefit enormously from the social time spent together too, especially with the way our **buy one, give one** model works – our courses bring people from all parts of the community together and create lasting friendships.

FAVOURITE DISH

Geelrys
(page 62)

18

Reuben Carr

MARKETING AND
EVENTS COORDINATOR

When I started looking for a job, I was hoping to find a company that was socially responsible – so Bounceback immediately stood out! I loved that the focus was completely on helping people and the **buy one, give one** model really struck a chord too.

It's wonderful to see people take part in our cookery courses and watch their confidence grow as they begin to believe in themselves. A personal highlight was helping Ben, who was learning to cook for his mother who had fallen ill and couldn't prepare their meals anymore. It was brilliant to see the joy on his face when he realised how simple it was to cook with fresh ingredients – he was so excited and proud to show her what he had learnt!

FAVOURITE DISH

Mung Bean Dahl

(page 36)

Ashton Coates

TECH DIRECTOR

Since joining Bounceback Food CIC, I have focused on working out how we can use 'tech for good' to scale up the core social impact that our organisation delivers regularly in the North West and Wales. The result of this has been the development of our recently launched Cooking and Nutrition Portal, which is enabling individuals and organisations to get 24/7 access to our range of healthy recipes, meal planning tips, budgeting advice and nutritional support across the UK.

I've also helped to build our website, online shop and crowdfunding campaign video. In the last few months I've been supporting our sister social enterprise, Bounceback Education too, by creating an online tutoring platform that's connecting teachers with pupils from Salford to Kenya!

FAVOURITE DISH

Sticky Pak Choi

(page 42)

Libby Element

Libby Element is a self-taught artist based in Manchester. She uses acrylic paint to bring her favourite subjects to life and is obsessed with light, shade and texture. Libby has been selling art prints on Etsy since 2014 and also sells her work at various art fairs in the Manchester area.

As a longtime vegetarian, this project has been close to Libby's heart as our recipe book features exclusively vegetarian and vegan recipes. Although Libby's work has been published online and in various publications, this will be the first book Libby has illustrated.

FAVOURITE DISH

Phở

(page 40)

20

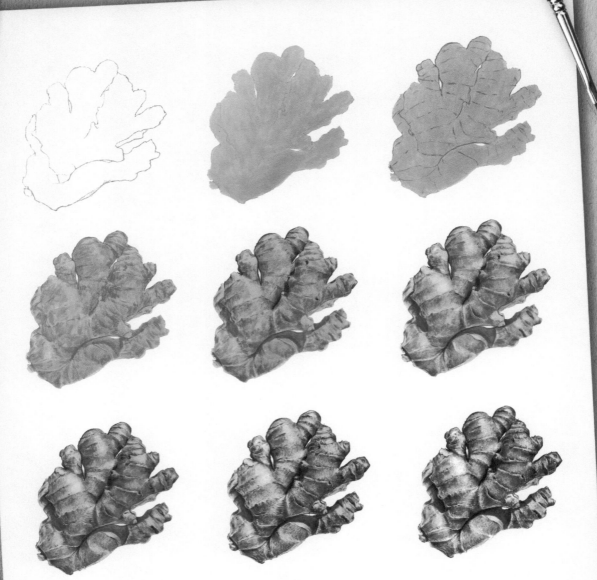

Phở
(page 40)

What **UNITES** people is the fact that

 *everyone is learning* something **different**.

It doesn't matter if you've bought a  TICKET

or are there for **FREE**  People from **all backgrounds** in the same community

come together to create a beautiful meal and share

the joy of **cooking**

HOW THE COURSE WORKS

Using a **buy one, give one** model to teach people a range of *Secret dishes from around the world* ensures that all members of the community can take part in the cookery course. Every ticket sold funds a free place for someone referred to us from a local third sector organisation – including foodbanks, charities and sheltered accommodation providers.

We welcome people of all ages and abilities. No previous cooking experience is required. Our experienced course tutors provide hands-on support and accommodate all learning needs in a friendly, supportive environment.

Not knowing the nationality of food you're going to cook on the evening adds an extra level of excitement! Meeting people from all walks of life and creating new friendships adds to the whole experience.

For a full list of our upcoming public cookery courses, head to the Bounceback Food website:

www.bouncebackfood.co.uk

WHO WE HELP...

Michael

Michael was referred to us from Middlewich Foodbank. His wife had always been the chef of the family but when she sadly passed away in late 2017, he was left in the unfamiliar position of having to cook his own meals. In his own words,

"Having only ever peeled a potato – this was quite a struggle!"

However, after completing several of our cookery courses in Sandbach, Michael is now full of confidence and has the skills to cook a range of healthy meals from scratch!

FAVOURITE DISH

Koshari

(page 46)

Clare was referred to us from CAP (Christians Against Poverty) in Altrincham. She was receiving debt management support, after a divorce that left her having to take on temporary jobs and use credit cards to support her 3 children. Clare had always been a good cook, but was bored by making the same low budget meals over and over again. However, on our courses Clare has been able to learn how to make a variety of cost-effective, exciting meals from around the world that have reignited her passion for cooking!

FAVOURITE DISH
Gigantes Plaki
(page 56)

Clare

Dave

Dave was referred to us by The Welcome Centre in Knutsford. He was born with cerebral palsy and as a result lacked confidence in his cooking ability, mainly due to the fear of having an accident. Dave was happy that we were able to include him in the courses and says he has regained his confidence with using kitchen knives thanks to the help and support we have given him with his technique.

FAVOURITE DISH

Coconut Kaukau

(page 70)

Nicola joined us on one of our first community cookery courses in Knutsford after buying a ticket from our market stall.

"I had never been on a cookery course before but loved the idea of learning to cook new and interesting dishes as I felt, as a family, we had got stuck in a rut. The added bonus of my ticket funding a place for someone else was the icing on the cake. It was fabulous to meet new people from all walks of life, to share the experience and wonderful food. What a great combination!"

FAVOURITE DISH

Injera
(page 50)

Nicola

HANDY TOOLS & ALTERNATIVES

In this section, our chef Josh shares his thoughts on a selection of kitchen utensils that can help improve your cooking!

Spatula, Tongs and Spoons

When buying these kitchen essentials, you'll need to consider how frequently you'll use them – and remember what they're best for! Spatulas are essential for pancake style flipping and are useful for scraping stuck food from the bottom of a pan. Tongs are good for flipping bits of vegetable in the pan but not as good for trying sauces. Spoons are great for tasting and stirring sauces but can make it difficult to flip things e.g. onion slices which can stick flat to the pan.

You'll also need to consider the material utensils are made from. Metal and plastic tools are more hygienic and easier to clean. However, if a plastic tool is not heat resistant it can melt on a hot surface. Metal tools can damage the bottom of a pan when used incorrectly.

Knives

One well suited, versatile knife, looked after, will serve you much better than a whole set of specialist blades. When choosing a knife consider how comfortable you are with its weight and size. We recommend a medium to semi-large chef's knife as a good, all purpose home kitchen option. Small knives will struggle to chop more hardy vegetables and a larger, heavier knife can be a little cumbersome and tiring to hold if you are not used to them.

Pans

One or two medium sized saucepans will see you through most dishes in our Cooking and Nutrition Portal. Every cuisine in the world makes use of pan frying and so it's worth finding one you can use over and over for different sized dishes. We recommend opting for a saucepan with a lid, which can be used for stocks, soups, pasta and rice as well as frying vegetables.

Spice Mixers

For the strongest flavours, grinding spices fresh with a pestle and mortar is usually best. One made out of stone will work as well as other more expensive (granite) options, they are relatively cheap too. Once bought they will last a lifetime and they can really help bring your dishes to life! If you don't have a pestle and mortar, you can mix together pre-ground herbs in a bowl with a teaspoon instead.

Blenders

While the price of some premium blenders can reach astronomical heights, simple hand blenders can be found for about £5-10 in most larger supermarkets or appliance retailers. These handy little tools are great for liquifying soups, curries and purées. A half decent one will also make quick work of awkward tasks like chopping nuts, though this can also be achieved by careful chopping with a knife. Blenders with a chamber fitting are also excellent for making pesto.

Although blenders are perhaps not quite a kitchen essential, they are certainly worth considering especially if you find the labour of excessive chopping difficult or if you are cooking for someone who struggles with solid foods.

INDIA

RED LENTIL &
SPINACH MASALA

A SPICE SENSATION. MAKE YOUR OWN CURRY FROM SCRATCH

SERVES
3-4

CURRY

1 tsp olive oil

1 red onion, diced

1 garlic clove, crushed

4 handfuls of spinach
leaves

400g tin chopped
tomatoes

Masala paste (see right)

450ml vegetable stock

200g red lentils

MASALA PASTE

2 tsps garam masala

2 tsps chilli powder

2 tsps smoked paprika

1 tsp cumin

1 tsp coriander

1 tsp ginger

1 tbsp vegetable oil

2 tbsps tomato purée

Salt and pepper to taste

TIPS

Goes well with low-fat
natural yoghurt and a
chapati or roti.

METHOD

1. Begin by preparing the masala paste in a pestle and mortar until well combined and smooth.

2. For the curry, heat the oil in a large frying pan, add onion and cook until softened, for around 3-4 minutes.

3. Add the crushed garlic and cook for a further minute.

4. Add the masala paste and cook on a low heat to release the flavours.

5. Add the chopped tomatoes and vegetable stock, bring to the boil.

6. Add the lentils, reduce heat and simmer for 20 minutes, stirring occasionally.

7. Remove from heat and add spinach leaves, allowing them to wilt with the warmth. If necessary, loosen with a little more stock.

MUNG BEAN DAHL

AN ANCIENT INDIAN RECIPE THAT'S BELIEVED TO HAVE HEALING PROPERTIES

SERVES
3-4

INGREDIENTS

½ leek, finely chopped

1 garlic clove, crushed

½ thumb size piece of ginger, peeled and grated

1 tbsp olive oil

1 tsp mustard seeds

1 tsp cumin seeds

½ tsp ground turmeric

½ tsp ground cinnamon

1 medium tomato sliced and diced

1 tsp chilli powder

Juice of 1 lemon

250g mung beans, soaked overnight in cold water

500ml of vegetable stock

Handful of fresh coriander

TIPS

Use fresh chillies for an extra kick of heat.

Works well with chutney, yoghurt and naan bread.

METHOD

1. Heat the olive oil in a pan over a medium heat. Add the mustard seeds and cumin seeds and fry until they start to pop.

2. Add the leek, ginger and garlic. Cook for 5-10 minutes or until soft and sweet.

3. Drain and rinse the mung beans then add to the pan together with 500ml of vegetable stock, turmeric and cinnamon. Bring to a medium simmer.

4. Add the roughly chopped tomato, chilli powder and chopped coriander stalks then leave all ingredients to simmer for 30 minutes or until the mung beans are tender.

5. Serve with a squeeze of lemon juice and sprinkle the coriander leaves on top.

VIETNAM

PHỞ

AN AUTHENTIC DISH THAT'S FULL OF NUTRIENTS AND BOLD FLAVOURS

SERVES
4

VEGETABLE PHO

1 portion of broth (see right)

2 carrots, peeled then thinly sliced

1 pak choi

1 red chilli, thinly sliced

1 lime, halved

100g noodles

150g mushrooms, sliced

Handful of beansprouts

Handful of coriander

Handful of basil

Handful of mint leaves

BROTH

1 litre of vegetable stock

1 cinnamon stick

1 star anise

1 tsp fennel seeds

4 cardamom pods

1 tsp coriander seeds

8 whole black peppercorns

1 thumb size piece of ginger, peeled and grated

Handful of fresh coriander

TIPS

Use courgette noodles as a vegan alternative

METHOD

1. Add all ingredients for the broth in a saucepan and bring to the boil, simmering for 15 minutes.

2. Boil the noodles for 3-4 minutes, then remove from the pan and drain under cold water. Place in your serving bowl together with the beansprouts and chilli.

3. Strain your broth into a large bowl, discarding the solids, then return the liquid to the saucepan, bringing it to the boil.

4. Add the mushrooms, carrots and pak choi stalks to your broth. Cook for 1-2 minutes then add the pak choi leaves.

5. Finish by ladling the broth over your noodles. Garnish with the chopped herbs and a squeeze of lime.

STICKY PAK CHOI

THE PERFECT, TASTY SIDE DISH

SERVES
3

INGREDIENTS

1 red onion, chopped

2 thumb size pieces of
   ginger, peeled and
   grated

2 tbsps vegetable oil

3 garlic cloves, crushed

3 tbsps light soy sauce

Juice of 1 lime

250g pak choi, halved or
quartered

TIPS

The cooking process is
quick so it's useful to have
all ingredients to hand.

Add chilli flakes if you
like heat!

METHOD

1. Pour the oil into a pan and get to a high temperature.

2. Carefully place the pak choi into the pan, cut-side down. Cook without
   stirring until they take on a light brown colour but remain crisp. Remove
   from the pan when cooked and set aside on a plate.

3. Add more oil to the pan then add the onion and ginger. Cook for 2-3
   minutes before adding the garlic.

4. Put the pak choi back into the pan together with the soy sauce. Cover with
   a lid and let them steam for 1 minute.

5. Take off the lid, remove the pan from the heat and serve with lime juice.

EGYPT

KOSHARI

A STREET FOOD SENSATION FROM EGYPT

TOMATO SAUCE

3 tbsps vegetable oil
2 red onions, diced
3 garlic cloves, crushed
1 tbsp white wine vinegar
500ml passata
Salt and pepper to taste
Baharat spice mix
(see page 81)

KOSHARI

1 litre vegetable stock
4 cardamom pods,
    cracked
1 tbsp olive oil
1 brown onion, sliced
200g green lentils,
washed
200g basmati rice,
washed
100g macaroni

TIPS

Add some freshly chopped
parsley on top to garnish.
Some people also like to
add chickpeas to this dish
for extra protein!

METHOD

1. Add half of the vegetable oil to a pan on a high heat, then fry the brown onion slices until crispy. Remove from the pan and leave to one side on a layer of kitchen roll to dry and cool.

2. Next, place the lentils in a large pan and cover with 500ml of stock. Bring to the boil then reduce to a low heat. Stir occasionally, and add water if necessary.

3. Now add the remaining vegetable oil to a separate pan on a medium heat. Add the red onion and a pinch of salt. Cook for 5 minutes until soft. Add the garlic and cook for 2 minutes.

4. Reduce the heat and add the Baharat spice mix, stirring frequently. Add the passata and vinegar. Cook for 10 minutes, then remove from the heat.

5. In a new pan add the rice, 500ml of stock, cardamom pods and olive oil. Bring to the boil then put the lid on and reduce to a low heat.

6. Remove excess liquid from the lentils when cooked. Once the rice is cooked, combine with the lentils and keep the lid on to maintain heat. Reusing the empty rice pan, add the macaroni and cover with water and a pinch of salt. Cook until al dente, drain the water and leave to one side.

7. Give the sauce a 1 minute blast of heat then combine the elements by creating a base layer of rice and lentils, with the macaroni and sauce on top. Sprinkle with crispy onions.

ETHIOPIA

INJERA

A SOFT, SPONGY FLATBREAD THAT CAN BE USED TO SCOOP UP STEWS OR VEGETABLES

SERVES
4 - 5

INGREDIENTS

250g self-raising flour, sieved

70g of whole wheat flour, sieved

70g cornmeal

1 tsp active dry yeast

500ml of water

TIPS

Injera works as an accompaniment to a whole range of dishes, including our aubergine and chickpea wat (see page 52).

When cooking you shouldn't need to turn the flatbread, but ensure the bottom doesn't burn by adjusting the heat if necessary.

METHOD

1. Sieve both types of flour and the cornmeal into a large mixing bowl.

2. Add yeast and mix together.

3. Next, slowly add the water, mixing as you go until a batter forms.

4. Place this in a sealed container and leave in the fridge overnight.

5. The next day, return the batter to a large mixing bowl and loosen with a dash of water if required.

6. Using a ladle, add a portion of batter to a pan over a medium heat.

7. Leave over the heat until the injera is fully cooked on top and browned on the base.

AUBERGINE & CHICKPEA WAT

THE RICH, WARMING FLAVOURS OF THIS DISH
ARE BEST ENJOYED WITH FRESHLY MADE INJERA

INGREDIENTS

1kg red onions, diced

4 eggs

3 garlic cloves, crushed

1 thumb sized piece of
ginger, peeled and
grated

1 tbsp of butter

500ml vegetable stock

200ml of vegetable oil

125g aubergine, sliced

400g of chickpeas, washed

Berbere spice mix
(see page 81)

Salt to taste

TIPS

This recipe is much milder
than the original Ethiopian
dish, so if you want the
authentic experience, add
some chillies for extra
heat.

METHOD

1. Boil the eggs for 6 minutes then transfer to cold water. Once cool, peel and then
   place to one side.

2. Add 2 tbsps of vegetable oil to a large pan over a medium heat. Add the onions and
   a dash of salt. Cook for 10 minutes or until soft.

3. Add the rest of the oil and cook for a further 5 minutes. Add the garlic and ginger,
   stir and cook for 5 minutes.

4. Add the Berbere spice mix. Mix thoroughly and cook for 10-15 minutes, ensuring
   that none of the spices remain dry.

5. Next add the butter and stock, mix and leave to cook for 10 minutes.

6. Now add the aubergine and chickpeas. Place a lid on the pan and cook for a further
   10 minutes. Add the eggs then cook for a final 2 minutes before serving.

GREECE

GIGANTES PLAKI

LOW IN FAT, THIS CAN BE ENJOYED EITHER AS A SIDE DISH OR A MAIN MEAL WITH BREAD

SERVES
4

INGREDIENTS

2 tbsps of olive oil

½ red onion, chopped

1 carrot, diced

1 garlic clove, crushed

½ tsp paprika

400g tin of butterbeans, drained and rinsed

400g chopped tomatoes

200ml of water

2 tbsps of tomato purée

2 tsps of dried oregano

Handful of spinach

Handful of fresh parsley

Handful of fresh mint leaves

TIPS

Serve with pitta bread or a crisp, green salad.

METHOD

1. Heat the oil in a large, lidded pan. Add the finely chopped onion and carrot. Once softened slightly, add the garlic and paprika then cook over a medium heat for 2-3 minutes.

2. Add the butterbeans to the pan followed by the chopped tomatoes and water.

3. Add the purée, oregano and season well. Bring the mix to the boil and then lower the heat so the stew is simmering and put the lid on. Leave to simmer for 15-20 minutes.

4. Chop the spinach roughly and add it to the stew, letting it cook for 2 minutes with the lid off.

5. Stir through the chopped parsley and mint before serving. Taste and adjust seasoning if required.

SOUTH AFRICA

CHAKALAKA

A DELICIOUS, LOW FAT SOUTH AFRICAN CHILLI

INGREDIENTS

1 tbsp olive oil

½ red onion, finely chopped

3 garlic cloves, crushed

1 red chilli, finely chopped

1 tbsp mild curry powder

1 pepper, finely chopped

2 medium carrots, peeled and grated

1 tbsp tomato purée

1 tbsp BBQ sauce

2 thyme sprigs, leaves only

1 thumb-sized piece of ginger, peeled and grated

400g tin of haricot beans, drained

400g chopped tomatoes

250ml of water

TIPS

Sprinkle coriander on top to garnish.

Substitute haricot beans for a tin of baked beans if preferred.

Serve with rice or extra veg for a full meal.

METHOD

1. Heat oil in a medium-sized pan. Add the onion and cook until soft.

2. Stir in the garlic, chillies and ginger. Cook on a low heat for 1-2 minutes, then add the curry powder and stir to make a curry paste. Add water if required.

3. Stir in the peppers and cook for 2 minutes more. Add the carrots and stir to make sure they're coated in the curry paste.

4. Add the purée, chopped tomatoes, BBQ sauce and thyme.

5. Add the haricot beans and water. Bring to the boil, reduce the heat and simmer for at least 10 minutes until the vegetables are tender and the mixture has thickened.

GEELRYS

THIS DISH HAS ITS ROOTS IN THE DUTCH EAST INDIES AND WORKS WELL WITH CHAKALAKA

INGREDIENTS

1 tsp turmeric

1 cinnamon stick

1 tsp ground cinnamon

600ml of water

300g long grain rice

60g sultanas

Salt and pepper to taste

TIPS

Replace water with stock
for extra flavour.

METHOD

1. Add the water (boil first to save time) to a large saucepan and bring to the boil.

2. Wash the rice then add to the water, together with all the other ingredients.

3. Mix thoroughly and season, then cover with a lid. Simmer for 15-20 minutes, stirring occasionally.

4. Remove from heat and set aside for another 5 minutes, keep the lid on.

5. Remove cinnamon stick then use a fork to fluff the rice before serving.

BRAZIL

BLACK BEAN FEIJOADA

A VEGGIE VERSION OF BRAZIL'S NATIONAL DISH

SERVES
4

INGREDIENTS

2 400g tins of black beans, drained

1 bay leaf

1 tbsp olive oil

1 red onion, chopped

1 green pepper, finely diced

3 garlic cloves, crushed

½ tbsp paprika

½ tbsp ground coriander

½ tbsp ground cumin

1 tsp cumin seeds

1 tsp cinnamon

½ tsp dried oregano

1 litre vegetable stock

125g chopped tomatoes

Handful of coriander

Juice of 1 lime

Salt and pepper to taste

TIPS

Serve with tortilla chips or freshly made guacamole.

Add sliced jalapenos for extra heat.

For a thicker soup, only blend ⅓ of the beans.

METHOD

1. Heat the oil in a large pan over a medium heat, then add the onion, pepper, garlic and salt. Cook, stirring for 2-3 minutes until the onion starts to soften.

2. Add the spices, oregano and bay leaf then cook for 1-2 minutes.

3. Add the drained black beans, stock and chopped tomatoes. Bring to a simmer and cook for 30 minutes until the beans are very soft.

4. Transfer half of the mixture into a large bowl, using a ladle. Use a hand blender to smooth, then pour back into the pan and stir well.

5. Add the chopped coriander and lime then cook for a further 5 minutes. Check the seasoning and adjust if necessary before serving.

PAPUA NEW GUINEA

COCONUT KAUKAU

SWEET POTATO, KNOWN AS KAUKAU IS A STAPLE OF THE LOCAL DIET

SERVES 4

V

INGREDIENTS

4 medium sweet potatoes

1 tbsp butter

3 tbsps grated fresh coconut

200ml coconut milk

½ red onion, finely chopped

2 garlic cloves, crushed

1 thumb size piece of ginger, peeled and grated

2 tbsps fresh orange juice

Salt and pepper to taste

TIPS

Add more coconut milk if you can't get hold of a fresh coconut.

METHOD

1. Pre-heat the oven to 200°C.

2. Rinse the sweet potatoes then wrap individually in foil. Bake for 50 minutes or until cooked through.

3. While you wait, combine the fresh grated coconut, coconut milk, orange juice, onion, garlic and ginger in a bowl, mix well.

4. Remove the sweet potatoes from the oven and cut lengthways. Scoop out ¾ of the sweet potato into a bowl. Immediately add the butter, salt and pepper then mash with a fork until you get a smooth purée.

5. Add the purée to your pre-prepared coconut mix. Stir thoroughly then fill the hollowed half sweet potatoes with the mashed mixture.

6. Bake in the oven for another 5-10 minutes until you have crispy skins.

STOCK

MAKE YOUR OWN STOCK TO ADD A GREATER
DEPTH OF FLAVOURS TO YOUR DISHES. IT'S ALSO
AN EXCELLENT WAY TO USE UP SPARE VEGETABLES,
HELPING YOU TO REDUCE FOOD WASTE.

ASIAN VEGETABLE STOCK

THIS VERSATILE STOCK CAN BE USED AS THE BASE
FOR A VARIETY OF SOUPS AND IS FULL OF FLAVOUR

INGREDIENTS

3 sticks of celery, roughly
chopped

2 carrots, roughly
chopped

2 brown onions, halved

4 garlic cloves, whole

1 thumb sized piece of
ginger, roughly chopped

3 star anise

2 cinnamon sticks

2 tsps of peppercorns

4 cloves

2 tsps salt

2 tbsps vegetable oil

3 litres of water

TIPS

Any old vegetables at the
bottom of your fridge can
be thrown in too, which is
a great way to cut down
on food waste!

METHOD

1. Add the oil to a large pan over a medium heat and fry the onion, carrot and celery until they are lightly charred.

2. Add the water and bring to the boil then reduce to a medium heat and add all the other ingredients listed above.

3. When the stock is boiling, add the lid and leave simmering for 2½ hours.

4. Using a sieve, separate the liquid from the other ingredients. Discard the vegetable remains as they will be tasteless. Use your stock as required.

EUROPEAN VEGETABLE STOCK

THIS STOCK IS PERFECT FOR SOUP AND GRAVY

INGREDIENTS

3 litres of water

3 sticks of celery, roughly chopped

1 carrot, roughly chopped

2 brown onions, halved, skin on

3 garlic cloves, halved

Handful of rosemary

Handful of thyme

TIPS

Add extra herbs of your choice to create your own signature stock.

METHOD

1. Add the oil to a large pan over a medium heat and fry the onion, carrot and celery until they are lightly charred.

2. Bring to the boil, then reduce to a medium heat and add all the other ingredients.

3. Cover with a lid and leave to reduce for 2½ hours.

4. Using a sieve, separate the liquid from the other ingredients. Discard the vegetable remains as they will be tasteless. Use your stock as required.

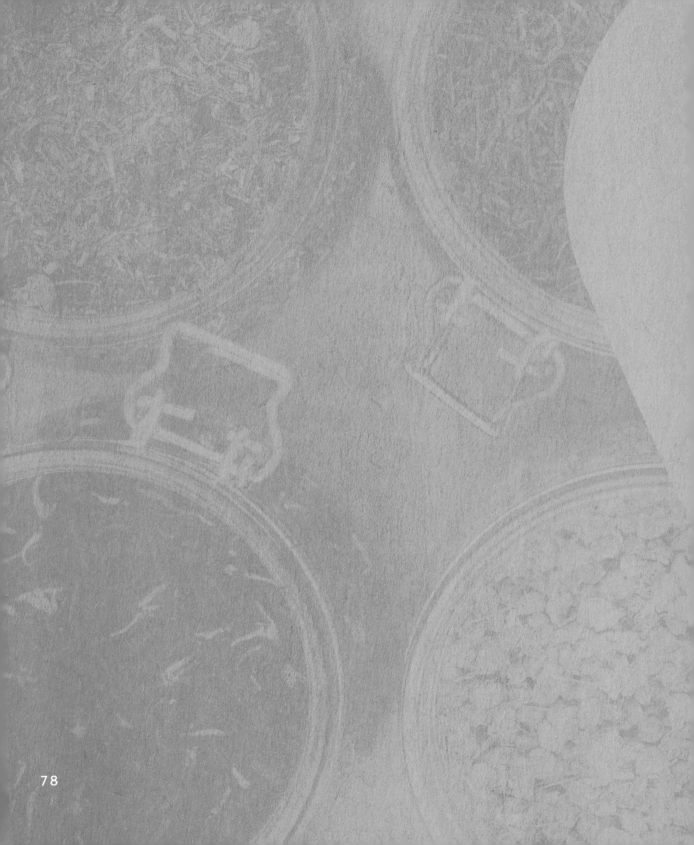

SPICE MIXES

THESE ARE BEST MADE WITH A
PESTLE AND MORTAR AND WILL MAKE
YOUR DISHES MORE AUTHENTIC.

BERBERE SPICE MIX

INGREDIENTS

2½ tsps ground coriander
4 tsps smoked paprika
1 tsp ground cumin

3 tsps cinnamon
½ tsp fenugreek
3 cardamom pods

METHOD

1. Burst cardamom pods to reveal the seeds, discard the shells.

2. Combine the seeds with the remaining spices into a bowl and mix.

BAHARAT SPICE MIX

INGREDIENTS

1 tbsp black peppercorns
1 tbsp cumin seeds
2 tbsps coriander seeds
1 tsp ground cinnamon

1 tsp chilli powder
1 tsp ground nutmeg
1 tsp smoked paprika

METHOD

1. Dry fry the cumin and coriander seeds until warm. Transfer to a pestle and mortar and crush.

2. Combine with the remaining spices into a bowl and mix.

Join us ON the ROAD less travelled

As we head into the next decade, our community cookery school will need to adapt continually to meet the needs of millions of people still living in food poverty in the UK.

Our response will always be proactive, with the **buy one, give one** model at the core of how we support people, either with the emergency provision of food or as a means of teaching people how to cook.

We're also embracing tech so that we can provide support to people 24/7 in the North West and beyond via our Cooking and Nutrition Portal. The platform enables people to access recipes, budgeting support, nutrition advice, cooking tips and meal planning guidance in their own time. Already, over 10,000+ licenses have been allocated to people since its launch in the summer of 2019!

There are so many ways in which you can support our development over the next few years too! Signing up to become a member of our cookery school (see page 84) will give you access to the recipes in our Cooking and Nutrition Portal. You may also like to take part in our corporate 'cook off' challenge (see page 86) or why not book us in to host a supper club (see page 87)?

All of the above will help our organisation to grow over the next few years and support more and more people through the power of social enterprise.

Thank you for your continued support.

Much love,
The Bounceback Team

JOIN OUR COMMUNITY COOKERY SCHOOL AND HELP US GROW

Recipes from 25+ countries

New exciting recipes every month

Plan your next secret dishes adventure

Improve your budgeting and batch cooking skills

Simple to use, wherever you are

Save and share your favourite dishes with your friends and family

You will also get

Invites to exclusive member only events

Discounts on merchandise in our online store

To sign up, visit:

www.bouncebackfood.co.uk/membership

CORPORATE CHALLENGE

Take on our Cook Off and support our community cookery school.

Go up against another business/organisation in your sector or battle it out amongst yourselves!

How it works

2 teams of 6 employees (half for the kitchen, half for front of house) cook for 12 additional guests who you feed and serve throughout the night. Our team organises your evening in partnership with our hosts, the Cheshire Cookery School. At the end of the evening we judge all of the dishes and decide who wins!

Help us grow

We ask all participating businesses/organisations to make a 'pay as you feel' donation to help cover the costs of the evening and further the development of our community cookery school.

Team building with a twist

SUPPER CLUBS

Celebrate diversity

How it works

Invite your friends round for a dinner party with a difference, as our amazing team serve up a feast of exciting recipes from around the world!

We provide all the food, you provide the drinks and guests.

All we ask is that you make a contribution to the development of our community cookery school.

For all bookings and enquiries email: info@bouncebackfood.co.uk

Meal Planner - Monday

Breakfast

Lunch

Dinner

Snacks

Notes

Meal Planner - Tuesday

Breakfast

Lunch

Dinner

Snacks

Notes

Meal Planner - Wednesday

Breakfast

Lunch

Dinner

Snacks

Notes

Meal Planner - Thursday

Breakfast

Lunch

Dinner

Snacks

Notes

Meal Planner - Friday

Breakfast

Lunch

Dinner

Snacks

Notes

Meal Planner - Saturday

Breakfast

Lunch

Dinner

Snacks

Notes

Meal Planner - Sunday

Breakfast

Lunch

Dinner

Snacks

Notes

INDEX